Shining the Light on The Secret

Shining the Light on The Secret

Andy Kaufman

Shining the Light on The Secret
Copyright ©2007 by Andy Kaufman
Published by Zurich Press

Second edition, November 2007
ISBN 0-9720587-2-9

Contents

THE TRUTH WILL SET YOU FREE

"What is truth?"
Pontius Pilate, John 18:38

Sue picks up her decaf soy latte and takes a seat on a comfy chair near her good friend Trish. They're finally able to carve out some time to catch up on each other's lives.

Eventually the conversation leads to a book that Sue just finished reading.

"This book can change your life, Trish. It's amazing! I couldn't put it down!"

Trish is intrigued. One part skeptic and two parts open to life change, she asks, "What book is that?"

*"It's called **The Secret**. It's written by Rhonda Byrne from Australia. I'm sure you've heard about it. Everyone's reading it or watching the DVD. Didn't you see it on Oprah?"*

*Trish chuckles as she admits it's been quite a while since she's taken time to tune in Oprah. "So... what's so amazing about **The Secret**? What's it about?"*

"It's all about the Law of Attraction. You know, you reap what you sow. Stuff like that. But it's more than just positive thinking. It's like science and it goes way back to some of the most successful people ever. Trish, this stuff even helps get parking spots."

"Parking spots?"

"Absolutely! They talk about it in the book. And as I was driving here today, I tried it. I concentrated real hard on getting a good parking spot. And guess what? When I showed up, I got one pretty close. Trish, I think this Secret stuff really does work!"

Trish wonders. "Hmmm.... Does it get New Agey? I'm always a bit concerned that things like this are at odds with our religious views."

> *"Not to worry!" Sue assures. "'You reap what you sow.' That's in the Bible. Just like 'God helps those who help themselves.' It's totally OK for us Christians."*
>
> *Trish smiles at her enthusiastic friend, two parts interested in learning more and one part realizing her friend may not know the Bible quite as well as she might think....*

WHAT IS TRUTH?

When the latest *secret* to success flies across your radar screen, how do you know if it's really true? Jesus proclaims in the Bible that "the truth will set you free."

Yet it's fair to ask the question Pilate put before Jesus, "What is truth?"

It's not a trivial question. And the way you answer it impacts nearly every aspect of how you view the world around you.

YOUR WORLDVIEW

Everyone has a worldview. We have presuppositions that influence our outlook on life. A worldview is like a set of lenses which taint our vision or alter the way we perceive the world around us.[1]

SHINING THE LIGHT ON THE SECRET

The term worldview may sound rather theoretical or philosophical, "a topic discussed by pipe-smoking, tweed-jacketed professors in academic settings."[2] However, "a person's worldview is intensely practical…. Our choices are shaped by what we believe is real and true, right and wrong, good and beautiful. Our choices are shaped by our worldview."[3]

Nearly every person eventually wrestles with four of life's ultimate questions:
- Who am I?
- What am I to do while I'm here?
- What's wrong with the world?
- How can what's wrong be made right?

How would you answer those questions? On what would you base your answers?

Ultimately your *worldview* provides the answers. But on what is your worldview based?

Few people consciously develop their worldview in a strategic, thoughtful way. Typically it's formed over time by influences such as our upbringing, education, and the culture around us. When pressed to defend what they believe, many people find it difficult to put together a rational argument. They just believe it.

That was certainly my story for many years. I was like the vast majority of Americans who believe in God[4]. If asked, I would readily state that I believed the Bible is literally true (which put me in good company. According to a recent Rasmussen

Reports poll, 54% of all Americans believe the Bible is literally true.[5])

Yet what I lived out in my daily life was based at least as much on what I had been taught by my parents and teachers, and fed by movies and the culture around me. Let's face it: I am a Cubs fan because I grew up with a dad who loves the Cubs, certainly not because of their long history of World Series wins!

In recent years I've taken worldview significantly more seriously. I've studied with great interest the differences between worldviews, and cherish extended discussions with people I meet who actively live out worldviews quite different from my own.

I eventually came to the conclusion that the only worldview I was willing to bet my life on was Biblical Theism, which uses the Bible as the source for answers to man's problems. I found the others insufficient in their answers and often requiring far more faith than basing my life on the best selling book of all time[6] (and I'm not talking about **The Secret**)!

A BIBLICAL WORLDVIEW RESPONSE

The purpose of this book is to look at **The Secret** through the lenses of a Biblical worldview.

Perhaps you already own **The Secret**. Or it could be you're attracted to its messages based on what you've heard from others, but you'd like a Biblical perspective on it. Or maybe a friend or family member gave you this book because they care about you and want to share some insights into their worldview.

It could be you're already feeling a bit skeptical about this book being based on the Bible, feeling a sense of "I've already tried that." You don't *have* to buy into a Biblical worldview to get value out of this book. At the least I trust you'll better understand the benefits and dangers of Rhonda Byrne's work.

Beyond that, I pray you'll also have a better appreciation for the importance of a worldview that is based on more than cultural influences and sincere intentions. And who knows? You might just find out that the Bible more rationally explains the world around us than you thought.

Are you completely satisfied with your answers to questions such as:
- Is there a God? If so, what is this God like?
- How do I know if something is right or wrong?
- What gives meaning to life?
- How did life begin?
- Is there life after death? If so, what will it be like and how can I influence my destiny?

May this be another step in your journey to more thoroughly developing a worldview that helps you answer those questions. And may this journey bring you the peace, meaning, and true success that drew you to **The Secret** in the first place.

QUESTIONS FOR DISCUSSION

- What is a worldview?
- How would you answer the four ultimate questions (see page 6)? On what do you base your answers?
- What are some influential factors that have shaped your worldview? How often do you consciously consider it?
- If you bought the book or movie, what were your motivations for doing so? What did you want to get from it? If you haven't read or watched **The Secret** but are considering doing so, what do you want to get from it?

Chapter 2

THE LAW OF ATTRACTION

"A man reaps what he sows."
Galatians 6:7

"OK, Sue, so tell me more about this Law of Attraction thing. I'd love to attract some new customers for my home business!"

"I hear you! My wish list is pretty big as well! In the book it talks about homes, cars, all kinds of things that people were able to attract!"

Trish is thirsty for another sip, and more information. "So how does it work?"

"It's like what we've heard in church for years, Trish. You reap what you sow. Ask and you will receive. The author even quotes the Bible."

"Really?" Trish asks.

"Yep. I even dog-eared the page. Let's see... Here, on page 47. Remember when Jesus talked about believing our prayers so much that we can send a mountain into the sea? That's the Law of Attraction!"

"So it's prayer?"

"Well, not exactly, I guess. It's thinking really intently about what you want. The author and some of the guests in the book talk about making sure you visualize what you want with so much focus that you feel it at an emotional level."

Trish recalls hearing similar ideas in a seminar on goal setting. "That makes sense. It's not really prayer, but is somewhat similar.... You think about what you want, focus on it with persistence, and you get it. But can it be that simple?"

*Sue nods enthusiastically, "It really is! In fact, **The Secret** says that the Universe is required to give it to you. Like the Bible... it doesn't say 'Ask and you might receive!'"*

"The Universe?" Trish wonders.

> *"Yeah, that's what the author calls it. I think that's just her politically correct way of talking about God. But doesn't this stuff make sense? If you're rude to prospects—like that would ever happen—but if you were, doesn't it make sense that they'll probably not become customers? But if you treat them with kindness and love then it comes back to you?"*
>
> *"That does make sense," Trish admitted.*
>
> *"I think so, too," replied Sue. "Whether it's customers, cars, or parking spots, you get what you attract. That's the Law of Attraction."*

Type "Law of Attraction" (with quotes) into Google and you'll find at least 1,500,000 results. Follow a couple of these and you'll uncover some interesting interpretations of what it means.

One site says the "Law of Attraction (LOA) is the most powerful force in the universe."[7] Phrases associated with the law include:

- Like attracts like
- Whatever you want, wants you
- What you put out, you get back
- Thoughts turn into things
- What you sow, you reap

The Law of Attraction generally says you create your own reality through your thoughts. Change how you think and you change your reality.

In some ways, the Law of Attraction aligns with what we observe in life. If you are kind to other people, they tend to be kind back to you. If you consistently display an angry disposition, you can count on similar crabbiness in return.

IS IT JUST THE RULE OF RECIPROCATION?

Interestingly, extensive research has been done on what Robert Cialdini calls the Rule of Reciprocation in his engaging book entitled **Influence: Science and Practice** (Allyn & Bacon).

The Rule of Reciprocation says we are inclined "to repay, in kind, what another person has provided us…. By virtue of the reciprocity rule, we are obligated to the future repayment of favors, gifts, invitations, and the like."[8]

Cialdini further explains how intensive research found the rule to transcend cultures, with evidence of its existence in all human societies.[9]

Pay for a friend's lunch and she feels compelled to pay next time. Open the first set of doors to a building for a person and he's inclined to open the second set for you. Give the prospect a free trial, and they can feel compelled to buy from you.

Sociologists and anthropologists confirm one of the most widespread and basic norms of human culture is embodied in the rule for reciprocation.[10]

Could it be that respectful words being returned as kindness is really just this reciprocity rule in action rather than the Law of Attraction?

OR PERHAPS CONFIRMATION BIAS?

Confirmation bias occurs when we selectively focus on evidence that tends to support what we want to be true while discounting or ignoring evidence which would contradict or disprove those beliefs.

As an executive coach, I've seen many leaders over the years make decisions to enthusiastically go forward with projects that eventually fail miserably. Often we can trace the root causes of the failure back to confirmation bias: the executive only considered evidence that supported the decision while ignoring the facts shouting "Don't do this project!"

The fortune cookie says "You'll encounter a mysterious stranger today," and with a little help from confirmation bias that stranger is destined to be found!

Whether it's the result of a fortune cookie, horoscope, or the Law of Attraction, one should at least be careful that it's not just a classic case of confirmation bias at work.*

BUT WAIT, THERE'S MORE!

Taken figuratively, the Law of Attraction means we can feel better about our situations by changing how we think. Or we could use it as an inspiration, that by believing we will succeed, we will perform better in a race or a test or our relationships.[11]

The Secret is, however, going further than just inspiration, reciprocity and confirmation bias.

> *"Its explicit claim is that you can manipulate objective physical reality— the numbers in a lottery drawing, the actions of other people who may not even know you exist—through your thoughts and feelings."*[12]

How does this happen? Dig far enough into the philosophies of many who preach the gospel of the Law of Attraction and you'll find there's more behind the "Universe" than simply a politically correct reference to God.

---

* I realize atheists often accuse Bible-believing Christians of exercising confirmation bias when it comes to creation, prayer, and other aspects of our faith. After much consideration of alternatives, I still maintain that the Biblical theism worldview offers the most reasonable answers for life's ultimate questions. Faith is required, but it is not a blind faith, and atheists who point the finger of confirmation bias must carefully look into the mirror as well.

THE LAW OF ATTRACTION

In **The Secret**, the "Universe" is always spelled with a capital U, implying an intelligence or force that is something quite different from just the typical meaning of the entire cosmos: everything that exists, including the Earth, planets, stars, galaxies, and all that they contain.

In fact, on page 157 the author gets more specific and calls it the "Universal Mind." Throughout the book it's clear this so-called "Universe" is an impersonal force that blindly obeys the commands of people who understand the Law of Attraction.

There's nothing new about the idea of the Universal Mind. It's a central doctrine of the New Age Worldview (see Appendix A: Worldview Comparisons).

A core component of The New Age Worldview is monism: all is one. The cosmos is pure, undifferentiated, universal energy and everything within it is one vast, interconnected process.

This worldview thus sees humans, nature, the earth—everything—infused with or of the same essence as God. Everything that is, is God. Philosophers refer to this as pantheism.

The number of American followers of so-called New Thought churches hovers around 200,000. They attend one of hundreds of loosely affiliated metaphysical churches that have been around for more than a century, with guiding principles anchored to self-fulfillment through the power of the mind.[13]

As with much New Age thought, it's easy to sneak past the guard post of our mind because of the alluring elevation of self, tolerance, and enlightenment.

After all, isn't it more enlightened to think that all religions are essentially One? Regardless of whether it was Jesus, Buddha, Muhammad, or Krishna talking, weren't they basically saying the same thing? The New Age worldview replies, "Amen!"

If you read the book or watch the movie, be forewarned that, at its core, **The Secret** is New Age evangelism wrapped up in an attractive self-help package.

"Pantheism? Monism? Universal Mind? All I wanted was a way to be more successful." There's a reasonable chance you might be signing up for more than you bargained for if you buy into what **The Secret** is teaching.

WHAT DOES THE BIBLE SAY?

Certainly the Bible reinforces some aspects of what is considered the Law of Attraction.

Galatians 6:7-9 says:
> *Do not be deceived: God cannot be mocked. A man reaps what he sows. The one who sows to please his sinful nature, from that nature will reap destruction;*

the one who sows to please the Spirit, from the Spirit will reap eternal life. Let us not become weary in doing good, for at the proper time we will reap a harvest if we do not give up.

In Matthew 7:7-12, Jesus says:
Ask and it will be given to you; seek and you will find; knock and the door will be opened to you. For everyone who asks receives; he who seeks finds; and to him who knocks, the door will be opened. Which of you, if his son asks for bread, will give him a stone? Or if he asks for a fish, will give him a snake? If you, then, though you are evil, know how to give good gifts to your children, how much more will your Father in heaven give good gifts to those who ask him! So in everything, do to others what you would have them do to you, for this sums up the Law and the Prophets.

It's reasonable to think these New Testament passages weren't primarily focused on helping us attract new sports cars, bigger homes, and better parking spots.

In John 15:7, Jesus says:
If you remain in me and my words remain in you, ask whatever you wish, and it will be given you.

One measure of truly remaining in Him is that we're in tune with God enough to pray according to His priorities, not simply our own.

In Philippians 2:3-4, Paul teaches:
> *Do nothing out of selfish ambition or vain conceit, but in humility consider others better than yourselves. Each of you should look not only to your own interests, but also to the interests of others.*

THE SECRET'S WORLDVIEW EXPOSED

Even a casual reading of **The Secret** cannot avoid the focus on using the Law of Attraction to reap material possessions more than humility and character.

And what about this impersonal so-called "Universe?" On page 163, Byrne exposes more of her worldview:
> *The true supply is the invisible field, whether you call that the Universe, the Supreme Mind, God, Infinite Intelligence, or whatever else.*

This is not simple semantics. There is nothing in the Bible that would allow God to step down into that crowd of "whatever else."

The Bible speaks of a God who knows us personally and desires a personal relationship. God pursues Adam in Genesis chapter 3. Both the Old and New

THE LAW OF ATTRACTION

Testaments refer to a God who knows and desires to be known by his followers. The very covenant name of God, Yahweh, describes the God who enters into personal relationships (covenants) with individuals and with groups.

Contrast this to the New Age worldview: an impersonal field of energy vs. a personal loving God.

And the implications? If God is impersonal or *all is One*, there is no basis for absolutes in terms of truth, ethics or understanding reality.

"What is reality? What is truth? How do I know if something is right or wrong?" It's whatever a New Age believer perceives it to be.

On the surface this may seem harmless enough. Yet a logical extension of the philosophy leads to ethical relativism.

Richard Weaver's seminal book **Ideas Have Consequences** sought to communicate that ideas, and not just actions, have consequences that logically follow.

Despite the alluring promise of The Law of Attraction, the underlying principles which uphold the worldview have potentially staggering consequences just below the surface.

If all moral opinions and lifestyles are equally valid, how can we condemn a serial killer? A pedophile? A racist? Adolph Hitler?

Even Charles Manson understood the implications of ethical relativism when proclaiming "if all is One then nothing is wrong."

IN SUMMARY

There's no secret to **The Secret**. It asserts that the Law of Attraction allows your thoughts to control the "Universe" so you can get exactly what you want, every time, and it's available to anyone.

At the core of **The Secret** is a New Age worldview that is neither new nor a secret.

The Bible teaches that we reap what we sow, and invites us to approach God in prayer for what we desire.

Yet this loving God is not a blind genie answering "Your wish is my command." Instead, in His love for us He gives what is best for us, which is not always the same as our wish list.

There is a stark contrast between these worldviews. Before buying into the Law of Attraction, first understand the underlying foundations and the logical consequences of them.

Are there some ideas in **The Secret** that align with what the Bible teaches? The next chapter addresses that question.

QUESTIONS FOR DISCUSSION

- How would you explain the Law of Attraction to another person?

- What are some examples you've seen of the *Rule of Reciprocation* and *Confirmation Bias* in action?

- **The Secret** says "Trust the Universe. Trust and believe and have faith." (page 57). Which is easier for you to believe in and trust your fate to: an impersonal Universe that obeys the intentions of selfish people, or a personal God that loves us, desires relationship with us, and provides peace and hope and all that we need instead of all we want? Why?

REFLECTING THE LIGHT

"Whatever is true, whatever is honorable, whatever is just, whatever is pure, whatever is lovely, whatever is commendable, if there is any excellence, if there is anything worthy of praise, think about these things."
Philippians 4:8

"Sue, something I particularly like about these concepts is the emphasis on how we think. For example, I know with my new business that the more I think about how to be successful, the more focused I am on being successful. But when I get worried about making mistakes, I seem to make more of them."

"I've seen that in my own life as well," Sue admits. "I've heard that athletes use visualization to improve their performance. **The Secret** calls it playing 'make believe'."

> *"I've used affirmation statements before to help get my thoughts straightened out," Trish relates. "Before a sales call I tell myself, 'This is a great product. This product will help many people. I am excited about sharing the story about this product. I am a successful business owner', you know, things like that. I've found it helps me prepare."*
>
> *"I'm glad you're seeing some positive aspects to this whole Secret thing." Sue pauses. "Truthfully, I was concerned you'd think I was a little wacky to buy into it."*
>
> *"Oh, Sue... You know I love you regardless, even when you do get a little over the top with Oprah's latest recommendations! Yet I wonder... Do these ideas work because of some ancient secret, or do they work because they align with how God set things up?"*

Let me be clear upfront: I'm not recommending you go out and buy **The Secret**. The most valuable ideas in the book are not a secret and can be found in plenty of other sources that avoid the baggage we'll talk about in the next chapter.

But it is worth investing this chapter on some content in **The Secret** that *does* align with a Biblical worldview to help improve our discernment when future *secrets* come our way.

HOW WE THINK

The Secret agrees with what the Bible teaches: that our thoughts are critically important. Thoughts ultimately shape choices, which have consequences.

The Bible describes how evil desires can eventually lead to sinful choices, which can have devastating results:

> But each one is tempted when, by his own evil desire, he is dragged away and enticed. Then, after desire has conceived, it gives birth to sin; and sin, when it is full-grown, gives birth to death. (James 1:14-15)

Philippians 4:8 encourages us to focus our thoughts on the true and noble.

Our thoughts influence our feelings and our performance. An important principle of change from my book **Navigating the Winds of Change: Staying on Course in Business & in Life** (Zurich Press) is that we can change the way we feel by changing how we think.

Let's say you're in business and dread making sales calls. You can try *doing different things* to be more effective. For example, I have a friend who forces himself to make ten cold calls over the phone each day. He puts ten giant paperclips (any physical object can work) on his desk at the start of the day. Each time he makes a call, regardless of the outcome, he takes one of the paperclips off his desk. This visual reminder keeps him on track.

That *might* work for you, but what about changing *how you think* about making the calls in the first place?

Instead of allowing yourself to dread making the calls, what if you first worked on reframing the whole process? It's not a cold call; rather, it's a call to a person who has a problem that you can solve. Or perhaps you can think of it as a challenge—a skill that, over time, you want to master.

Seeing it differently can give you the motivation to *do things differently*.

Of course, that's quite different from saying we are powerful enough to turn *thoughts* into *things* every time, without fail, because of an "impersonal Universe."

The Bible teaches we can significantly limit what we can do by what we think. We can squander what we've been given (Matthew 25). It also shows us that great faith can lead to great results (Matthew 21:21 and Mark 11:23).

POWER OF VISUALIZATION

Visualizing a future event can help one prepare. It can be a powerful tool in preparing for a future action. Playing "make believe" (page 105 in **The**

Secret) can be a powerful way to change how we feel.

Sometimes our negative thinking or visualizing becomes a self-fulfilling prophecy. Earlier this week at my son's Little League baseball game, young Brady was assigned to be catcher in the next inning. While he was putting on the equipment in the dugout I heard him repeat over and over, "I hate catching! I hate catching!"

Overhearing this I replied, "Hey, Brady buddy! Try this: 'I love catching! I love catching!'"

He looked at me for a moment, and then went back to "I hate catching! I hate catching!"

Well, it soon became time to take the field. During warm-ups Brady looked pretty good. But sure enough, when the first pitch of the inning sailed toward the batter, the ball smacked Brady right in his face mask, totally missing his glove! I could imagine what Brady was mumbling to himself: "See! I told you! I hate catching!"

Motorcyclists are taught to beware of *target fixation*. If you focus on the big truck beside you, you'll tend to drift towards it. Some people, like Brady, focus on the negative and it pulls them head on into the outcome they fear.

Yet it can work *for* us instead of *against* us. I found visualization to be a powerful way to overcome a fear of speaking. I regularly speak to large groups of people but only a decade ago I would be stricken with fear if I had to stand up in front of a group as small as ten people!

The difference? There was much prayer involved. I also read a lot of books and committed to practicing. Finally, a key additional factor was visualizing before a presentation. What would the room look like? How would I say certain lines? How would I move around the room?

In a sense, I was playing 'make believe', fixating on the target of a great presentation. That technique, combined with all the education and prayer, keeps me rock solid when speaking in just about any context these days.

The Secret states this all works because visualization emits a "powerful frequency out into the Universe" (page 81). A Biblical worldview sees visualization working because it taps into the way God designed our brain and physiology. We are "fearfully and wonderfully made." (Psalm 139:14)

WE ARE NOT OUR CIRCUMSTANCES

It is so easy to slip into a victim mindset. When things go wrong, we can get stuck in the quicksand of believing we are powerless to act.

The Secret reinforces that we are not our circumstances. Things can change—in fact, plan on it! And we can be a part of the change. **The Secret** invites people to change by sending out different thoughts to the "Universe." The emphasis is on *intention* and *feeling* rather than *action*.

This approach can lead to not taking responsibility for "our part", leading to a victim's mindset (e.g. "I'm not going to work on my resume and go interview. Instead, I'm going to transmit 'high-paying job' thoughts to the Universe").

The Biblical worldview understands that God has given us a *brain* and *will* to do our part. We may have to extend forgiveness or show courage by taking steps outside our comfort zone. We may have to change our mind by focusing on the truth instead of ruminating on stories that may be based on lies.

We need to put off our old self (Ephesians 4:22-24), set our mind on the things above (Colossians 3:2), and renew our mind rather than conform to the pattern of this world (Romans 12:2).

We need to do *our* part while leaving *God's* part to Him.

THE ATTITUDE OF GRATITUDE

Gratitude—a sense of thankfulness—is powerful, and **The Secret** reinforces that the attitude of gratitude is abundantly important to our success.

Where a Biblical worldview differs from **The Secret** is *where* the gratitude is expressed (to God, not to the "One Universal Mind") and *why* (not to *get* things from the "Universe" but because I have been *given so much* by God).

I've grown to greatly appreciate a service called Send Out Cards (www.sendoutcards.com/23195). Since I spend a lot of time on the road, it's difficult to find time to look through cards at a store, find the one I want, and get it into the mail. Send Out Cards lets me do all that from my computer, using my own handwriting as the font.

In their materials they talk about the difference between "Give to Get" and "Give to Give". If you "Give to Get" (e.g. express gratitude as a way to get it back), it ends up being manipulative and insincere. "Give to Give" (e.g. expressing gratitude without a need to get it back) is so much more powerful. When **The Secret** speaks of gratitude, it appears to be more "Give to Get."

We have a greater impact on the world around us when we are characterized by an ongoing, daily spirit of "Give to Give" gratitude. Imagine relationships that flow with gratitude that is expressed without expectation of return.

The Bible encourages this in Colossians 3:14-16:
And over all these virtues put on love, which binds them all together in perfect unity. Let the peace of Christ rule in your hearts, since as members of one body you were called to peace. And be thankful.

THE POWER OF LOVE

The Secret says, "there is no greater power in the Universe than the power of love" (page 38). Pastor James MacDonald* once summarized love in a sermon as "You before me." We truly love someone else when we put *their* needs before *ours*, and that is, indeed, a powerful, life-changing action.

The Bible contradicts **The Secret**'s assertion that love is an impersonal force. The Bible says "God is love" (1 John 4:8, 1 John 4:16).

The Bible empowers us to truly love others because we see and experience how much God loves us.

THE POWER OF FOCUS

Focusing on goals is critically important to achieving results. Too often results are illusive because we do not set and doggedly pursue goals.

Yet this is not the result of an impersonal "Universe" blindly obeying our directives. Instead, it's reaping the result of sowing focused action.

Many find value in visibly posting pictures or slogans to keep focused on a goal. In my executive coaching practice I often find clients do not achieve goals because they forget about them in the midst of busy schedules. The visible

---

* Visit www.walkintheword.com to learn more about James MacDonald, Pastor of Harvest Bible Chapel Rolling Meadows

reminder (or a nudge from a coach) can keep one motivated to achieve desired goals.

None of this requires a genie-like "Universe" to blindly obey our wishes. On the contrary, it requires concentration and action on our part.

THE EFFECTS OF STRESS

We continue to learn how stress has a negative effect on our physiology. From impacting our ability to concentrate to triggering some diseases, too much stress can literally be deadly[14].

In the book of 1 Kings, chapter 19, the Bible relates a fascinating account of the prophet Elijah running from the evil queen Jezebel. What's remarkable is that Elijah had just won a miraculous victory over the prophets of Baal. One would think he would be fearless in the wake of seeing God deliver such an incredible victory.

However, a single threatening letter from Jezebel shows up and "Elijah was afraid and ran for his life" (1 Kings 19:3). After an extended time without sleep or food, Elijah hits rock bottom, even praying "Take my life" (verse 4). The story illustrates how stress can impact our ability to keep a healthy perspective.

Where the Bible differs from **The Secret** is that we don't have, as individuals, the divine power to be disease-free simply by thinking harmonious thoughts of perfection (as stated in the *Secret to Health* chapter).

In 2 Corinthians 12, the apostle Paul talks about a thorn in his flesh that tormented him.

> *Three times I pleaded with the Lord to take it away from me. But he said to me, "My grace is sufficient for you, for my power is made perfect in weakness."*

Paul's *intentions* were not enough to remove what most scholars agree was a physical ailment.

The Bible does not suggest that life on Earth will be free of disease, illness, or pain. In John 9:3, Jesus said a man's blindness "happened so that the work of God might be displayed in his life."

I realize that God allowing sickness, disease, and other suffering is an enormous hurdle for some to get over before pursuing a relationship with Him.[*]

Yet the Bible is clear that suffering is a fact of life. But it doesn't stop there: it promises that God is with us, and He provides help in the midst of the struggle.

---

[*] I recently had an e-mail conversation with an evolutionary philosopher regarding intelligent design. In short, he admitted his issue "is more theological than scientific." He doesn't like a God that allows bad things to happen and was therefore betting his life on an atheistic secular humanism worldview. His e-mail signature ended with the quote: "Nothing makes sense except in the light of evolution." Particularly if you assume there's no God.

Yale University psychologist Susan Nolen-Hoeksema includes *regular prayer* and *working on forgiveness* as helpful methods to quit worrying[15]—two topics the Bible is well prepared to address.

The Bible offers help during stressful times by repeatedly encouraging that we need not fear "for I am with you." (Genesis 26:24, Isaiah 41:10, Isaiah 43:5, Jeremiah 1:8, for example).

In Luke 12:6-7, Jesus encourages:
> *Are not five sparrows sold for two pennies? Yet not one of them is forgotten by God. Indeed, the very hairs of your head are all numbered. Don't be afraid; you are worth more than sparrows.*

Note the difference: it's a loving, personal God that pursues us, listens to our prayers, and provides comfort. His power, not some impersonal force, gives us the strength we need to persevere.

BE *FOR* SOMETHING

The Secret asserts we should not just be *against* something. We should be *for* something. It's not enough to simply be *against* hunger. What strategies do you support to help fight it?

However, **The Secret** is powerless in applying this principle as its recommendations boil down to thoughts, not actions.

Am I really *for* making this a better place if I'm unwilling to step out into the world and get my hands dirty?

IN SUMMARY

It would be easy to write-off **The Secret** as a ridiculous collection of empty, New Age philosophies revived through slick marketing. Yet millions of copies of the book are in print because a few concepts are close enough to the truth they remain palatable.

How we think matters. We reap what we sow. Visualization and focus are helpful allies in making life changes. We are not the sum of our circumstances. Gratitude and love are powerful. Stress needs to be managed. Be *for* something.

You don't need **The Secret** to reap the benefits of these concepts. They are fully available to those who live with a Biblical worldview.

QUESTIONS FOR DISCUSSION

- **The Secret** says "As I get out of bed, when one foot touches the ground I say, 'Thank,' and 'you' as my second foot touches the ground. With each step I take on my way to the bathroom, I say 'Thank you.' I continue to say and feel 'Thank you' as I am showering and getting ready. By the time I am ready for the day, I have said, 'Thank you' hundreds of times." (pages 75-76). To whom is the author saying "Thank you?"

- How have you used visualization to help in some area of your life? How is visualization similar to and different from prayer? Does visualization require the "Universe" of **The Secret**?

- What is one thing you could do differently if you thought about it differently?

THE DARK SIDE OF THE SECRET

"Dear friends, do not believe every spirit, but test the spirits to see whether they are from God, because many false prophets have gone out into the world."
1 John 4:1

"Here's something that I'm struggling with, Sue. I get that good things come to us because of good thoughts and intentions, and the reverse can be true as well. But how does that work with things like babies that get illnesses or tragedies like Darfur?"

Sue pondered Trish's question. "I hadn't really thought about that. It seems a little weak to say they were transmitting on the wrong frequency to the Universe, which is somewhat along the lines of what I recall from the book."

"And if I develop breast cancer, God forbid, was I somehow attracting that?"

Sue wrinkles her face, clearly showing she doesn't like what she's thinking. "Trish, there is a section in the book that talked about health and the Law of Attraction. It did seem pretty wacky, to be honest. One of the weight loss tips was to not look at fat people because it might cause you to think fat thoughts."

"You're kidding me, right?" Trish exclaimed.

"Uh, not really. There's definitely a theme in the book that medical problems stem from what we see and think. I'm not sure I totally buy that."

Both friends are quiet for a bit. Trish looks over and sees a portly bus driver heading their way with a large iced coffee drink and a giant cranberry muffin. She says in jest, "Take cover! 'Fat thoughts' incoming from the left!"

Sue and Trish both laugh, realizing it's clear this whole Law of Attraction thing can go too far.

DID THEY REALLY ATTRACT THAT?

The Secret's philosophy says that bad things, even great evils, happen to people because they are somehow on the same frequency as the event.

Those who lost homes or loved ones in Hurricane Katrina or other natural disasters were somehow attracting it. Jews killed in Nazi death camps were by some means on a very unfortunate frequency with the "Universe."

This single tenet of **The Secret** is outrageously repulsive, not even remotely comforting or empowering. Yet it is consistent with the New Age worldview.

"What is wrong with the world?" The New Age worldview responds, "You're sending the wrong signals to the Universe."

The secular humanism worldview answers the question with "Insufficient education or insufficient government." To make things better we just need to educate people or provide better government.

Would Hitler have acted differently if he had been better educated?

Would the effects of Katrina have been significantly mitigated if the Federal Emergency Management Agency (FEMA) would have been better run? Yes, for sure, but it doesn't explain it all. From the looting of stores to the "Lord of the Flies" environment in the Superdome, there were blatant examples of sin.

The Biblical worldview explains pain and suffering as the result of sin in the world. Why did God create us capable of sinning? Charles Colson addresses it at length in **How Now Shall We Live**. Here's a portion of his response:

Fair question. But think carefully about what it means. In order for God to ensure that we could not sin, he would have had to tamper with our freedom of will—to create us not as full human beings but as puppets or robots programmed to do only what he wanted. But that would have rendered us incapable of loving God or one another, for genuine love cannot be coerced. Also, without free will, we would not be capable of moral responsibility, creativity, loyalty, or heroism. The only way God could create beings that are fully human was to take the risk that they would use their freedom to choose evil.[16]

Many have told stories of great blessings emerging from times of deep suffering. Even in the darkness of a sinful world, we can see the love of a God who is ready and willing to help us.

THE "UNIVERSAL MIND?"

The Secret teaches the "Universe" is impersonal and blindly obeys our commands. The Bible teaches the enormous value in each person—we are made in the image of a loving, personal God.

The Secret says "the entire Universe emerged from thought." (page 15). Also, on page 143, "Everything in this world began with one thought."

42

Whose thought would that be? Is *thought* enough to create the complexity we see in a single cell?

There's an origins theory referred to as the *participatory anthropic principle*, which draws "a wild extrapolation from quantum mechanics. In short, it states that the universe did not fully exist until human beings emerged to observe it. And so, in order to become fully real, the universe decided to evolve human consciousness."[17]

Is that theory easier to buy into than believing an all-powerful God created this endlessly fascinating universe in all its complexity?*

FROM THE BIBLE?

The Secret says "the Creative Process ...was taken from the New Testament...", (page 47) perverting Matthew 21:22 and Mark 11:24.

These passages talk about praying with faith for amazing results, but they do not pre-suppose an impersonal force blindly responding. They assume a loving God who knows us intimately, desires relationship with us, who knows what we need and even withholds what we cannot handle.

---

* Perhaps you've written off the Biblical account of creation as a nice story but impractical in this scientific age. If so, you might be surprised how much faith is required with alternatives, including the Big Bang theory most of us grew up with. I recommend you check out www.AnswersInGenesis.org to learn more.

The Secret's assertion that the Creative Process is Biblical is offensive and far from the truth.

The Secret says "Abraham, Isaac, Jacob, Joseph, Moses, and Jesus were not only prosperity teachers, but also millionaires themselves, with more affluent lifestyles than many present-day millionaires could conceive of." (page 109).

Balance that with Jesus' statement:
> Foxes have holes and birds of the air have nests, but the Son of Man has no place to lay his head. (Matthew 8:20 and Luke 9:58).

Or in Luke 12:15 where he says:
> Be on your guard against all kinds of greed; a man's life does not consist in the abundance of his possessions.

Beware when people sprinkle a little Bible here and there to reinforce their unbiblical philosophies. The lack of context can twist the meaning, misleading the reader to false conclusions.

My friend Shane greatly respects a speaker and author who, as he communicates, uses verses of the Bible throughout his message. This speaker is also a major supporter of **The Secret** so when Shane found out about **Shining the Light on The Secret**, he was upset with me. The logic is something like this: "If someone mentions Bible verses and supports **The Secret**, then the Bible supports **The Secret** and we should not be concerned about what is being taught."

Don't be deceived. John instructs us:
> Dear friends, do not believe every spirit,
> but test the spirits to see whether they
> are from God, because many false
> prophets have gone out into the world.
> (1 John 4:1)

FAITH AND DEEDS

The Secret says:
> How the Universe will bring it [your
> intentions] to you is not your concern or
> job. Allow the Universe to do it for you.
> When you are trying to work out how it
> will happen, you are emitting a
> frequency that contains a lack of faith—
> that you don't believe you have it
> already. You think you have to do it and
> you do not believe the Universe will do it
> for you. (page 51)

This seems to absolve a person of responsibility to act. In the Biblical *reap what you sow* model, sowing is not simply passive faith.

James 2 talks about the relation of faith and deeds:
> Show me your faith without deeds, and I
> will show you my faith by what I do.
> (James 2:18)

The Secret quotes author and poet Horatio Bonar:

"Think truly, and thy thoughts shall the world's famine feed." (page 145).

On page 146, motivational speaker Lisa Nichols is quoted:

It's not your job to change the world, or the people around you. It's your job to go with the flow of the Universe, and to celebrate it inside the world that exists.

Can you imagine saying that to a civil rights activist? Where would we be today with slavery if people bought into this nonsense? Will our happy thoughts feed the poor in the streets of our cities?

James 2:15-17 says:

Suppose a brother or sister is without clothes and daily food. If one of you says to him, "Go, I wish you well; keep warm and well fed," but does nothing about his physical needs, what good is it? In the same way, faith by itself, if it is not accompanied by action, is dead.

The Bible spurs us to pray, to have faith in God, but also to take action.

CAREFUL WITH THAT QUOTE

The Secret quotes Alexander Graham Bell on page 84, "What this power is I cannot say. All I know is that it exists."

The implication is that he's talking about the power of attraction. The actual quote is:

> *"What this power is I cannot say; all I know is that it exists and it becomes available only when a man is in that state of mind in which he knows exactly what he wants and is fully determined not to quit until he finds it."*

This is quite different from sending thoughts and feelings to the "Universe". It speaks of determination and persistence.

The Secret quotes Winston Churchill saying "You create your own universe as you go along." That certainly sounds like Churchill is on board with the book.

That is until you look at the context of his statement. In his book **My Early Life** (1930), he writes:

> *Some of my cousins who had the great advantage of University education used to tease me with arguments to prove that nothing has any existence except what we think of it. The whole creation is but a dream; all phenomena are imaginary.* **You create your own universe as you go along**. *The stronger your imagination, the more variegated your universe. When you leave off dreaming, the universe ceases to exist.* **These amusing mental acrobatics are all right to play with. They are perfectly harmless and**

> **perfectly useless. I warn my younger readers only to treat them as a game**. The metaphysicians will have the last word and defy you to disprove their absurd propositions.[18]

Clearly Churchill was not spreading the gospel of **The Secret**. Rather, he was arguing against the very essence of **The Secret**'s message.

MOTHER THERESA HAD IT WRONG?

The Secret says,

> Many people have sacrificed themselves for others, thinking when they sacrifice themselves they are being a good person. Wrong! To sacrifice yourself can only come from thoughts of absolute lack, because it is saying, "There is not enough for everyone, so I will go without." Those feelings do not feel good and will eventually lead to resentment…. Your job is You. (page 118)

Imagine Mother Theresa living by **The Secret**. Imagine this being presented to patriots who sacrificed everything for their country.

Imagine a world where everyone's job is themselves. Think of the implications of this for parenting, Little League coaching, teamwork in the office, or being a firefighter or paramedic.

It's every man for himself, radiating happy thoughts to the "Universe." It's the ultimate in selfish hedonism.

Contrast this again with Philippians 2:3-4
Do nothing from selfishness or empty conceit, but with humility of mind regard one another as more important than yourselves; do not merely look out for your own personal interests, but also for the interests of others.

That mindset may not sell truckloads of self-help books but it has been a guiding principle for countless millions over the generations.

Love demands sacrifice. As stated before, true love is "You before me." It is sacrificial in that true love is willing to overlook wrongs, to see the good, to persist in trials.

Christ demonstrated the ultimate sacrifice of love:
...but God shows his love for us in that while we were still sinners, Christ died for us. (Romans 5:8)

YOU MUST LOVE YOU!

The Secret says:
The reason you have to love You is because it is impossible to feel good if you don't love You. When you feel bad about yourself, you are blocking all the love and all the good that the Universe has for you. (page 120).

(Note **The Secret**'s use of capital Y for "You".)

Bob Proctor, an author and long-time advocate of positive thinking adds to the "me" focus:
> I've been studying me for forty-four years. I wanna kiss myself sometimes!

Dr. Paul Vitz, Professor Emeritus of Psychology, NYU addressed this obsession in a talk entitled, "The Problem with Self-Esteem". He ends the talk:
> This narcissistic emphasis in American society and especially in education and to some extent in religion is a disguised form of self worship. If accepted, America would have 250 million 'most important persons in the whole world.' Two hundred and fifty million golden selves. If such idolatry were not socially so dangerous, it would be embarrassing, even pathetic. Let's hope common sense makes something of a come back.[19]

The Biblical worldview allows us to be content with who we are because God loves us—we are made in His image.

THE SECRET AND DISEASE

The Secret says:
> Disease cannot live in a body that's in a healthy emotional state. (page 130)

Later on the same page it argues (based on the fact that cells are being created all the time):

> *If our entire bodies are replaced within a few years, as science has proven, then how can it be that degeneration or illness remains in our bodies for years? It can only be held there by thought, by observation of the illness, and by the attention given the illness.... Illness cannot exist in a body that has harmonious thoughts.*

On page 131:

> *You can think your way to the perfect state of health, the perfect body, the perfect weight, and eternal youth. You can bring it into being through consistent thinking of perfection.*

Does human existence teach us that man is capable of perfect, harmonious thoughts that lead to eternal youth and disease-free living?

The Biblical worldview does not set perfection here on Earth as the goal. God can provide for us even in the midst of pain and suffering. The Apostle Paul repeatedly prayed for his affliction to be taken away, but the Lord replied, "My grace is sufficient for you, for my power is made perfect in weakness" (2 Corinthians 12:9).

The Secret says:

> *I believe and know that nothing is incurable. At some point in time, every so-called incurable disease has been*

cured. In my mind, and in the world I create, 'incurable' does not exist…. It is the world where 'miracles' are everyday occurrences. It is a world overflowing with total abundance, where all good things exist now, within you. Sounds like heaven, doesn't it? It is. (page 135).

The Bible's descriptions of heaven make Rhonda Byrne's version pale in comparison. As nice as her version might sound to some people, it's clear this world we live in is not heaven, despite whatever reality we attempt to conjure up in our mind.

THE SECRET'S WEIGHT LOSS PROGRAM

The Secret says:

if someone is overweight, it came from thinking 'fat thoughts'…. A person cannot think 'thin thoughts' and be fat. It completely defies the law of attraction.

It goes on.

Whether people have been told they have a slow thyroid, a slow metabolism, or their body size is hereditary, these are all disguises for thinking 'fat thoughts.' (page 58).

Further:

The most common thought that people hold, and I held it too, is that food was responsible for my weight gain. That is a belief that does not serve you, and in my

*mind now it is complete balderdash!
Food is not responsible for putting on
weight. It is your thought that food is
responsible for putting on weight that
actually has food put on weight…. Think
perfect thoughts and the result must be
perfect weight.* (page 59).

How we think can impact how and what we eat.
For example, when I'm under stress I tend to eat
more junk food.

But that's not what **The Secret** is saying. To the
contrary, it's saying that all weight problems are
manufactured by our thoughts, not our eating or
exercise habits (or medical conditions).

Psychologist John Norcross, a professor at the
University of Scranton and an authority on self-
help books:
*It's pseudoscientific, psychospiritual
babble…. We find about 10 percent of
self-help books are rated by mental
health professionals as damaging. This is
probably one of them. The problem is
the propensity for self-blame when it
doesn't work.* [20]

JUST STOP FIGHTING!

The Secret quotes Lisa Nichols:
*In our society, we've become content
with fighting against things. Fighting
against cancer, fighting against poverty,
fighting against war, fighting against*

drugs, fighting against terrorism,
fighting against violence. We tend to
fight against everything we don't want,
which actually creates more of a fight.
(page 141).

Did the Civil War create more slavery? Did World War II increase persecution and killing of Jews? Did the civil rights movement take freedoms away from minorities?

Are we really to think that the best way to deal with terrorism is to transmit happy, peaceful thoughts to the "Universe?" That certainly was not the terrorists' strategy on September 11, 2001.

The Bible certainly has themes of not resorting to violence, such as:
If someone strikes you on one cheek,
turn to him the other also. (Luke 6:29)

Yet a Biblical worldview allows room for fighting just causes.
There is...a time for war and a time for
peace. (Ecclesiastes 3:1,8)

In a world filled with sin, hatred, and evil, war is inevitable. Followers of a Biblical worldview should not desire war, but they are also directed to respect and obey the government God has placed in authority over them (Romans 13:1-4; 1 Peter 2:17). Perhaps the most important thing we can be doing in a time of war is to be praying for godly wisdom for our leaders, praying for the safety of our military, praying for quick resolution to the conflict, and praying for minimum casualties on both sides of the conflict.[21]

YOU ARE GOD

The Secret says:
> All that exists is the One Universal Mind, and there is nowhere that the One Mind is not. It exists in everything. The One Mind is all intelligence, all wisdom, and all perfection, and it is everything and everywhere at the same time. If everything is the One Universal Mind, and the whole of it exists everywhere, then it is all in You! (pages 160-161).

This asserts that God is everywhere and we are God, yet this "One Universal Mind" or God remains impersonal.

The Secret gets to the core of its worldview on page 164, including:
> "You are God", "You are God in a physical body", "You are Eternal Life expressing itself as You". "You are all power. You are all wisdom. You are all intelligence. You are perfection. You are magnificence. You are the creator, and you are creating the creation of You on this planet."

What evidence do we have of any human possessing all wisdom, all intelligence, and all perfection?

Simple observation makes it clear that we have trouble managing our own affairs, let alone being powerful enough to control the universe.

This worldview offers nothing beyond this life. In fact, what does **The Secret** enthusiastically say happens after death? Our energy remains eternal. That's comforting.

The Bible teaches a completely more satisfying message. The force holding everything together is not the "One Universal Mind," but the all-knowing, omnipresent, holy and loving God of the Bible. This same loving God has prepared a home in heaven for those who accept His gift of forgiveness.

Colossians 1:15-17 says:
> *He is the image of the invisible God, the firstborn over all creation. For by him all things were created: things in heaven and on earth, visible and invisible, whether thrones or powers or rulers or authorities; all things were created by him and for him. He is before all things, and in him all things hold together.*

In John 14:1-3, Jesus says (from *The Message*):
> *You trust God, don't you? Trust me. There is plenty of room for you in my Father's home. If that weren't so, would I have told you that I'm on my way to get a room ready for you? And if I'm on*

my way to get your room ready, I'll come back and get you so you can live where I live.

IT'S ALL ABOUT FEELINGS

The Secret says:
> *This is a feeling Universe. If you just intellectually believe something, but you have no corresponding feeling underneath that, you don't necessarily have enough power to manifest what you want in your life. You have to feel it.* (pages 52-53).

Later on page 53 the reader is instructed, "So feel good now." On page 61, "You must feel good." On page 85, "What's really important to the whole Secret is feeling good."

On page 100:
> *I want to let you in on a secret to **The Secret**. The shortcut to anything you want in your life is to BE and FEEL happy now!*

Jack Canfield says on page 178:
> *When I really understood that my primary aim was to feel and experience joy, then I began to do only those things which brought me joy. I have a saying, "If it ain't fun, don't do it!"*

Is the ultimate goal of life to feel good? If manifesting a *feel good* intention harms another person, is it still OK?

Ironically, this emphasis on feelings exposes a self-contradiction in **The Secret**'s worldview. Byrne contends we influence the "Universal Mind" through feelings, which are an intensely personal activity. Yet we're told the "Universal Mind" is impersonal, which seems to be a troublesome contradiction at best.

IN SUMMARY

The Secret is not a neutral book espousing harmless self-help tips. To buy into the Law of Attraction means you have to take the good and the bad from the "Universe." The book draws you into a worldview that says "You are god" and dangerously throws in a little Scripture to seek credibility. It risks disempowering people from taking action while removing their responsibility to do so in the first place.

Does the Bible have a secret that addresses our needs? That is the subject of the next chapter.

QUESTIONS FOR DISCUSSION

- **The Secret** says "You cannot harm others with your thoughts, you only harm You." How can that be? If the "Universe" blindly obeys my thought commands, what is the governor that limits the consequences to just me? If one's intentions are to feel good by having an affair (after all, "you deserve all good things life has to offer"), doesn't that reality harm your spouse?

- What are the ramifications of living a life of "If it ain't fun, don't do it?"

- What are the ramifications to society if we bought into the idea that sacrificing ourselves for others is wrong?

Chapter 5

THE BIBLE'S SECRET

"I have learned to be content whatever the circumstances. I know what it is to be in need, and I know what it is to have plenty. I have learned the secret of being content in any and every situation, whether well fed or hungry, whether living in plenty or in want. I can do everything through him who gives me strength."
Philippians 4:11-13

*"It's kind of funny to me, Trish. I feel like I got lured into the buzz about **The Secret** and didn't realize there were some pretty big implications and errors to the philosophies being preached."*

"Don't beat yourself up over it, Sue. You're in good company! It appears millions of others have been lured into the same hype."

"I suppose so. I'm just so surprised I didn't even detect that there were conflicts with my faith. How can that happen?"

"I don't know... It is a good reminder for us both to be a little more discerning when taking in the latest ideas."

"I agree. I need to spend more time getting a better understanding of the Bible and how I can live more true to its teachings. If something like this slipped in under my radar, chances are there's other stuff as well. I want my early warning system better prepared!"

"Well said. Sue, I think it's time we got moving. I'm starting to get some serious 'fat thoughts' about those apricot scones over there!"

"I'm with you! Now if only I could visualize a dinner for my family tonight!"

OUR APPETITE FOR ANSWERS

My friend Roger teaches high school level courses in a Michigan prison. Roger recently told me he's noticed an interesting trend among his students. There's this underlying belief that the reason *they* are in prison while *others* are free is because the people on the *outside* know some *secret*. They want Roger to help them understand that *secret* so they can get out and get ahead.

What is the secret to success? We have a hunger to know. Newsweek said it well regarding **The Secret**:

You'd think the last thing Americans need is more excuses for self-absorption and acquisitiveness. But our inexhaustible appetite for 'affirmation' and 'inspiration' and 'motivation' has finally outstripped the combined efforts of Wayne Dyer, Anthony Robbins, Dr. Phil, and Mitch Albom.[22]

In **The Secret**, the New Age Movement gets a new face and marketing arm, but it's really the same old message wrapped up into a brilliant package.

THE BOTTOM-LINE OF THE SECRET

Rhonda Byrne is so subtle in her message, starting out in a way that lures you in. But on the final page of the book, you get to its real message:

The earth turns on its orbit for You. The oceans ebb and flow for You. The birds sing for You. The sun rises and it sets for You. The stars come out for You. Every beautiful thing you see, every wondrous thing you experience, is all there, for You. Take a look around. None of it can exist, without You. No matter who you thought you were, now you know the Truth of Who You Really Are. You are the master of the Universe. You are the heir to the kingdom. You are the perfection of Life. And now you know The Secret.

THE GREAT LIE

Ultimately this is the great lie of Satan in the Bible.
*All this I will give you if you will bow
down and worship me.* (Matthew 4:9).

*"You will not surely die," the serpent
said to the woman. "For God knows that
when you eat of it your eyes will be
opened, and you will be like God,
knowing good and evil."* (Genesis 3:4-
5).

The *secret* is really just a re-telling of the ultimate
lie, that we don't need God. In fact, we *are* God.
It's a deceptively luring message, that sucked Eve
into the original sin, and whose gravity will pull in
many unsuspecting people looking for hope in a
book that promises it, but delivers the Ultimate Lie.

To an earlier point, it's not enough to just be
against **The Secret**. What am I *for*? What does
the Bible offer as an alternative?

THE REAL SECRET

There's a secret shared in the Bible that can
provide the peace and joy you just might be
searching for. You can find it in the New
Testament book of Philippians, chapter 4, starting
at verse 11:
*I have learned to be content whatever
the circumstances. I know what it is to
be in need, and I know what it is to have
plenty. I have learned **the secret** of*

being content in any and every situation, whether well fed or hungry, whether living in plenty or in want. **I can do everything through him who gives me strength**.

How many lives must we witness before we realize that *more stuff* and greater focus on ourselves are not the solutions for lasting contentment?

The Secret is filled with empty strategies promising more stuff. The Bible says you can be content regardless of what you have.

Moreover, you can have the strength to do everything you need, through Him. The "Him" is Jesus Christ, and He offers forgiveness, peace, joy, and an eternity in heaven, through a personal relationship with Him.

COMPARING THE WORLDVIEWS

So which worldview are you willing to bet your life on? Let's see how they answer the ultimate questions.

"Who am I?" The secular humanism worldview credits evolution with the answer. We're a random accident of natural processes run amok. The New Age worldview says we, along with everything around us, are part of the Universal Mind. *We* are god. The Bible says we are the crowning glory of creation, created by a loving God in His image.

"What am I to do while I'm here?" The secular humanism and New Age worldviews say we're here to consume and enjoy. Just be happy! Love yourself! Get what we can while we can, and why not tap into the Universal Mind so we can have even more to consume and enjoy? The Bible says we're here "for Him", to bring glory and honor to the Lord Jesus Christ. We don't exist for ourselves—to consume and enjoy—but rather to display His glory in the way we live.[23]

"What's wrong with the world?" Between the secular humanism and New Age worldviews, the problem is either education, government, or how we're interacting with the "Universal Mind." The Bible says the problem is sin. It's me. It's you. It's the sinful choices we make. Or others make. Or from the fact that we live in a sinful world.

"How can what's wrong be made right?" Better education or better government makes sense to a secular humanism worldview. "Better thoughts to the 'Universe'" is recommended by the New Age worldview. The Bible teaches we are reconciled to God because of the death and resurrection of Jesus. Out of love and grace He paid the price that I should have been required to pay for my own sin. It is a gift that cannot be earned, and that gift comes with peace, joy, an eternal future, and a personal relationship with Him that transcends anything that competing self-centered worldviews can serve up through their empty promises.

TAKING THE NEXT STEP

It could be you've already experienced this relationship and you've tasted the peace and contentment that comes with it. Your next step might be to more deeply understand your worldview so you're better armed against the lies the world bombards us with on a daily basis. In Douglas Groothuis book, **Unmasking the New Age**, he asserts:

> *Christians are partially responsible for the rise of the New Age. When and where Christians retreat, the enemy advances.*[24]

Appendix B provides some recommended resources to help you develop your Biblical worldview.

It could be you have no idea what a personal relationship with Jesus Christ means. In fact, when you hear about Jesus dying on the cross for your sins and having a personal relationship with Him it all sounds rather confusing.

Or it could be you feel like "I've tried the *church thing* and it didn't work." G.K. Chesterton wrote, "The Christian ideal has not been tried and found wanting; it has been found difficult and left untried." Could it be you tried *church*, but not *Christ*? Could I ask you to re-open your mind to the possibility that real answers are available to your questions?

I commend to you the best-seller that changed my life: the Bible. For years I considered the Bible to be a good book. But base my life on it? Is it accurate and reliable enough to stake my eternity on it?

If you're struggling to trust the Bible, I invite you to take action to investigate it. There are free resources such as "10 Reasons to Believe in The Bible" from RBC Ministries[25]. I also recommend you check out the free resources available at http://www.needhim.org.

Suggested books include Josh McDowell's **The New Evidence That Demands A Verdict Fully Updated To Answer The Questions Challenging Christians Today** and Lee Strobel's **The Case for Faith: A Journalist Investigates the Toughest Objections to Christianity**.

Get a Bible and start reading in the New Testament gospel of John. Find someone to whom you can ask honest questions and get straight answers.

If you pursue answers with an open mind, I pray you'll come to the conclusion that I did as well: that the Bible is trustworthy to bet your eternity on, that a loving God is pursuing you, and that the hope, peace, and joy you desire is available through the forgiveness of His Son's sacrifice on the cross and resurrection from the dead.

It's available to you right now, regardless of who you are and what you have done.

And now you know the *real* secret.

INVITATION

What questions or comments do you have after reading this book? I invite you to contact me at andy@ShiningTheLightOnTheSecret.com.

Also, visit the book's website at http://www.ShiningTheLightOnTheSecret.com for more resources and opportunities to discuss the book.

ACKNOWLEDGMENTS

This book was written because of Natalie Stacker, Vicki Bartotto, and Pam Babcock. Natalie planted the seed that a Biblical response to **The Secret** was needed, which gave me a hunger to learn more. Vicki was a participant in a workshop who raved about the book and was willing to loan it to me for a night. Notes from that evening turned into a blog entry sent to friends, family, and colleagues. Pam found out about it and suggested we turn it into a book. Thank you to each of you for your part in this work.

In addition to inspiration, Natalie provided invaluable editing input, as did Deb Gustafson and Warren Saufferer. You each made me a better writer. Special thanks also to Cindy Kiple for her expertise on the cover. To the many friends and family (such as my father Bill Kaufman, John Dreyer, Jon Lunde, and John Chmela) that read early drafts and provided encouragement along the way, thank you very much. Finally, thank you to my wife Sara and my children Barrett, Zachary, and Christa for their love, and for putting up with me reading it to them over the dinner table.

APPENDIX A: WORLDVIEW COMPARISONS

This table is adapted from the Worldview Chart by Summit Ministries (http://www.summit.org/resource/worldview_chart)

	Secular Humanism	Cosmic Humanism (New Age)	Biblical Christianity
Source	Humanist Manifesto I & II	Writings of Ferguson, Spangler; The Secret	Bible
Theology	Atheism	Pantheism	Theism
Philosophy	Naturalism	Non-Naturalism	Supernaturalism
Ethics	Ethical Relativism	Ethical Relativism	Ethical Absolutes
Biology	Darwinian Evolution	Darwinian/ Punctuated Evolution	Creation
Psychology	Monistic Self-Actualization	Collective Consciousness	Dualism
Sociology	Non-traditional, World State, Ethical Society	Non-traditional Home, Church, & State	Home, State, & Church
Law	Positive Law	Self-Law	Biblical/Natural Law
Politics	World Government (Globalism)	New Age Order	Justice, Freedom, Order
Economics	Socialism	Universal Enlightened Production	Stewardship of Property
History	Historical Evolution	Evolutionary Godhood	Historical Resurrection

APPENDIX B: WORLDVIEW RESOURCES

Recommended resources for developing a Biblical worldview include:

- **How Now Shall We Live**, by Chuck Colson.
- "Resources for Developing a Biblical Worldview", by Answers In Genesis. See http://www.answersingenesis.org/articles/am/v1/n1/developing-biblical-worldview. Note: this has a list of excellent resources for children and adults.
- Summit Ministries: http://www.summit.org. In particular, note their student and adult conferences, as well as workshops that can be tailored for schools and churches.
- World Magazine. This weekly magazine presents the news through a Biblical worldview. See: http://www.worldmag.com.
- Worldview Weekend. See their website at http://www.worldviewweekend.com for information about conferences and other resources.

REFERENCES

[1] "What is a Christian Worldview?"
http://www.christianworldview.net
[2] Colson, Charles. **How Now Shall We Live**,
Tyndale, p. 14.
[3] IBID, pp. 13-14.
[4] "Americans believe in God, with conditions", The
Washington Times, November 12, 2006
[5] "53% of Churchgoers Say Attendance is
Growing", Rasmussen Reports, July 19, 2006.
http://www.rasmussenreports.com/2006/July%20
Dailies/churchAttendance.htm
[6] Ash, Russell. **The Top 10 of Everything**. DK
Pub., 1996, pp 112-113.
[7] Author unknown. URL: http://law-of-attraction-
info.com
[8] Cialdini, Robert B. **Influence**, Fourth Edition,
Allyn and Bacon, 2001, p 20.
[9] IBID, p 20.
[10] IBID, p 50.
[11] Adapted from "Decoding 'The Secret'" by Jerry
Adler, Newsweek, March 5, 2007, p 54.
[12] IBID, p 54.

[13] "Secret history of 'The Secret'", Marco R. della Cava, USA Today, March 29, 2007, p D1.
[14] "Brooding weighs on mind and body: How you handle stress could be shortening your life", Marilyn Elias, USA Today, May 8, 2007, page 7D.
[15] IBID.
[16] Colson, Charles. **How Now Shall We Live**, Tyndale, p 213.
[17] IBID, p 65.
[18] As quoted at URL: http://henry.pha.jhu.edu/churchill.pdf
[19] "The Problem with Self-Esteem", Paul C. Vitz. URL: http://www.catholiceducation.org/articles/education/ed0001.html
[20] "Decoding 'The Secret'" by Jerry Adler, Newsweek, March 5, 2007, pp 56-57.
[21] Adapted from "What does the Bible say about war?", URL: http://www.gotquestions.org/war-Bible.html
[22] "Decoding 'The Secret'" by Jerry Adler, Newsweek, March 5, 2007, p 53.
[23] "How to Do Good So That God Gets the Glory", by John Piper, August 3, 1980, www.desiringgod.org.
[24] Groothuis, Douglas R. **Unmasking the New Age**, Downers Grove, Ill. InterVarsity Press, p174. 1986.
[25] Available for free online at URL: http://www.rbc.org/bible_study/ten_reasons_to_believe/reasons/7342.aspx

www.ingramcontent.com/pod-product-compliance
Lightning Source LLC
Chambersburg PA
CBHW071421040426
42445CB00012BA/1246